A Morning in South Wedge

DATES IN THE STATES

A COUPLE TRAVELING THE UNITED
STATES ON A BUDGET

Mystery Date
Rochester, NY

By Dates in the States

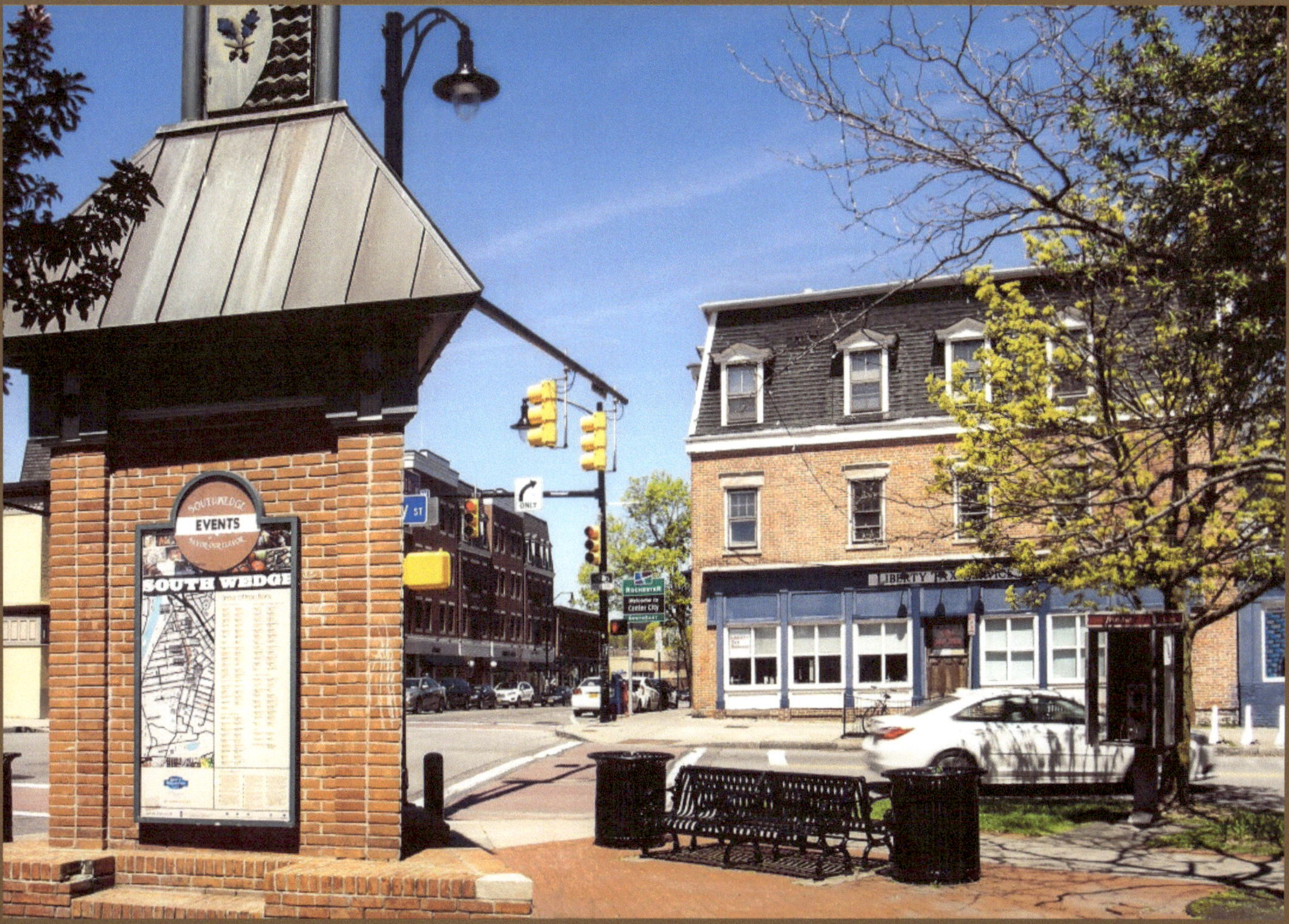

"Our passion is travel, and we want to share our adventures to inspire others to explore the world with their loved ones. Dare to live beyond the box."

Dates in the States

Introduction

Hey there! We're Crystal and Shane, the duo behind Dates in the States, a blog that's all about discovering adventure, connection, and fun in every corner of the U.S. From local events and hidden gems to restaurant reviews, invigorating hikes, and quirky roadside attractions, we're up for anything!

This South Wedge Mystery Date Book is your guide to a perfect morning in one of Rochester's most vibrant neighborhoods. Start your day with a refreshing yoga class to wake up your body and mind. Afterward, grab a cup of coffee at a cozy local café before strolling down South Avenue, where eclectic shops and historic charm make for the perfect browsing experience. Pick up a few unique finds, then stop by a market to grab fresh ingredients for a delicious meal you'll cook together at home.

Join us on this mystery date and uncover the charm of the South Wedge—where local culture, community, and creativity come together for a truly unforgettable morning!

Start

Tru Yoga
683 South Ave,
Rochester, NY 14620

Start your morning mystery date with movement and mindfulness at Tru Yoga, a welcoming studio in the heart of the South Wedge. With a variety of classes running from 6 AM to noon, you can choose the perfect session to energize your body and set a peaceful tone for the day ahead. Whether you're looking for a gentle flow or a dynamic vinyasa class, Tru Yoga offers affordable options for all levels.

Book your class in advance at truyogaroc.com and get ready to stretch, breathe, and unwind before diving into the rest of your South Wedge adventure!

Second Stop

Coffee Lover?

Coffee Connection

681 South Ave,
Rochester, NY 14620

Love coffee? Then be sure to stop by Coffee Connection! After your yoga session, recharge with a cup of locally roasted coffee from this cozy café with a heart. More than just serving great coffee, Coffee Connection empowers women in recovery from addiction, trauma, and incarceration by offering employment, training, and a supportive community. With every sip, you're supporting a fresh start for someone in need.

Prefer tea? Flip to the next page for an alternative stop!

Alternative Stop

Tea Lover?

Happy Earth Tea

696 South Ave,
Rochester, NY 14620

Prefer tea? Skip the coffee and head over to Happy Earth Tea for the ultimate tea experience! Known as one of the top tea spots in the U.S., this cozy haven offers a wide selection of loose leaf teas, expertly blended for the perfect brew. Whether you're a tea aficionado or new to the world of tea, Happy Earth Tea provides an inviting atmosphere to explore flavors, learn about tea, and enjoy a relaxing moment.

Take a sip and get ready to continue your South Wedge adventure!

Third Stop

Marilla's Mindful Supplies

661 South Ave,
Rochester, NY 14620

If you're passionate about reducing plastic waste and living a more sustainable lifestyle, you'll love Marilla's Mindful Supplies. This gem of a shop is dedicated to providing eco-friendly alternatives for everyday household and beauty products. What's even better? You can bring in your own jar or pick up one of their free jars available in-store, and fill it to your heart's content!

And let's not forget their secret treasure: the best candy around! Trust us, it's a must-try. More people need to know about it!

Take a moment to browse their selection, fill up your jar, and grab a treat. You'll leave with eco-friendly products in hand and a smile from the candy you can't stop thinking about.

Fourth Stop

Little Button Craft

658 South Ave,
Rochester, NY 14620

Step into Little Button Craft, a charming shop filled with locally made gifts, handcrafted goods, and unique finds from Rochester's most talented makers. Whether you're searching for a one-of-a-kind souvenir or just browsing for inspiration, this creative space is full of treasures waiting to be discovered.

And if you spot one of our Mystery Date Books inside—snap a selfie and share it on social media! Don't forget to tag us (@datesinthestates) so we can see your South Wedge adventure unfold.

When you leave Little Button, continue walking North down South Avenue and explore a few of the other shops along the way.

Fifth Stop

Abundance Food Co-op

571 South Ave,
Rochester, NY 14620

End your walk at Abundance Food Co-op, Rochester's only community-owned grocery store! Nestled in the heart of the South Wedge, Abundance is committed to offering local, organic, sustainable, and socially responsible products—so you can feel good about everything you put on your plate.

Now, it's time for a fun challenge: Pick Your Ingredients! Each of you will choose one ingredient that must be used in tonight's meal. Will it be a fresh, local veggie? A unique spice? Something unexpected? Get creative and make it your own!

Once you're home, cook up a delicious meal together to cap off your perfect day of adventure, connection, and good food.

Final Stop

Cheesecake anyone?
Cheesy Eddie's
602 South Ave,
Rochester, NY 14620

As you make your way back to your car near Tru Yoga, you'll stroll past Cheesy Eddie's—and if you love cake, this is your sign to stop! Treat yourself to the perfect dessert to enjoy after your home-cooked meal (if it makes it home that is!).

One of our all-time favorite spots, Cheesy Eddie's is famous for its rich, creamy cheesecakes and, in our opinion, the best carrot cake in Rochester. Moist, flavorful, and topped with the perfect layer of frosting, it's a sweet way to end your South Wedge adventure!

Final Stop

Chocolate Lover?

Hedonist Artisan Chocolates

674 South Ave,
Rochester, NY 14620

If you're craving something extra indulgent to cap off your day, Hedonist Artisan Chocolates is the perfect final stop. Located near the end of your adventure, it's a delightful treat for anyone with a sweet tooth.

Known for their handcrafted chocolates, Hedonist offers everything from rich truffles to unique confections, each one better than the last. If you're in the mood for something a bit more refreshing, their ice cream is absolutely to die for.

Whether you choose to end your date with decadent chocolate or want to visit both Hedonist and Cheesy Eddie's, it's the perfect way to add a sweet touch to your South Wedge mystery date!

Add Your Photos

Keepsakes

Thank you for joining us on this mystery date adventure! We hope you've enjoyed the delightful experiences and memorable moments we've crafted just for you in Webster, NY.

But the adventure doesn't stop here! Keep exploring exciting myste dates in other cities and uncover new romantic experiences across the U.S. by visiting our website, DatesInTheStates.com. There, you can purchase both physical copies and digital downloads of our mystery date books. Plus, don't miss out on our Mystery Date Book Club, where you can receive a brand-new mystery date book every month!

Tag us in your date photos on social media! @datesinthestates

About the Creators

Crystal, the writer and creator, is a storyteller at heart. When she's not uncovering hidden gems for the next date night idea, she runs her own digital marketing company, helping small businesses improve their content marketing, increase visibility in their communities, and streamline their online presence.
Visit: crystalstatskey.com

Shane, her husband and partner in adventure, is a dedicated personal trainer and the owner of Beekstar Fitness in Irondequoit, NY. He specializes in working with clients who have limited mobility, helping them build muscle and focus on pain areas so they can regain strength and confidence in their daily lives.
Visit: beekstarfitness.com

Crystal and Shane have explored every U.S. state except Alaska (coming soon!) and are now visiting countries in alphabetical order. Whether road-tripping or curating Mystery Date experiences, they're always chasing their next adventure.

Want to be featured?

MYSTERY DATE BOOK PACKAGES

—

Are you a small business looking to reach new customers? Feature your business in our next Mystery Date Book! Choose from our partnership packages below to connect with couples seeking unique experiences and exclusive deals.

Package One

LOCAL LOVE LISTING

—

A quick shoutout to show you're part of the neighborhood vibe.

Listed in the "Local Love" section of your designated neighborhood date book

Includes business name, address, and social link

Optional: Offer a small promo (e.g., 10% off for book holders)

1 social media shout-out when the book launches

$45

Package Two

FEATURE STOP

—

You're not just a business— you're part of the experience.

Marked as a "Must-Stop" on a Mystery Date

Full-page feature in the book with your story, offerings and photo

Includes 1 social media feature — a dedicated post and story highlighting your business

Note: To ensure each feature is genuine and experience-based, we require a hosted visit prior to inclusion.

$95

Package Three

PARTNER & SELLER

—

Be the spot and the source.

Everything in Tier 2

PLUS: Option to sell the Mystery Date Books at your location

Includes a bulk purchase of 10 books (yours to price + sell)

Keep 100% of the profits from in-store sales

Bonus: Tag as an official pickup location in our promotions

$150

Prices are subject to change

Feel free to reach us at any time by sending us an email to say hi and to learn more! We look forward to hearing from you.

| www.datesinthestates.com | datesinthestatesblog@gmail.com |

Sponsors & Affiliates

Our sponsors and affiliates help make our adventures possible! Explore the amazing brands and businesses that support our community.

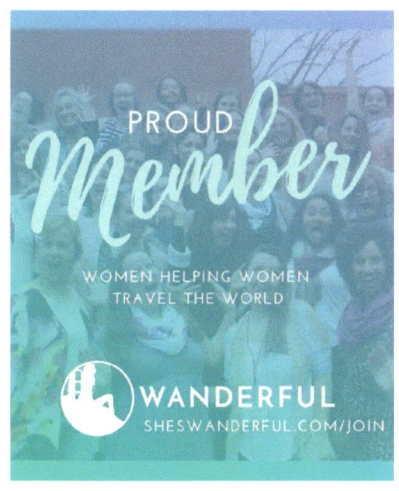

Wanderful

Wanderful is a global community for women who love to travel. Connect, explore, and join a local hub near you!

Join our Book Club!

Join our Mystery Date Book Club and be part of a travel-inspired community, discovering unique local adventures together!

HomeExchange

HomeExchange lets you swap homes with travelers worldwide for authentic, affordable stays. Join today and travel differently!

Shop our books at a store near you!

Little Button Craft
658 South Ave.
Rochester, NY 14620

The Pawsitive Cat Cafe
120 East Ave. Ste 100
Rochester, NY 14604

Yesterday's Muse Books
32 West Main St.
Webster, NY 14580

Writers & Books
740 University Ave,
Rochester, NY 14607

Littleberger Florist
63 North Avenue,
Webster, NY 14580

Flight Wine Bar
262 Exchange Blvd,
Rochester, NY 14608

Scents by Design
728 University Ave,
Rochester, NY 14607

Union Tavern
4565 Culver Rd,
Irondequoit, NY 14622

DATES IN THE STATES

A COUPLE TRAVELING THE UNITED
STATES ON A BUDGET

Contact Us

🌐

datesinthestates.com

datesinthestatesblog@gmail.com

📍

Based in Rochester, NY

CONNECT WITH US ON SOCIAL!

@DATESINTHESTATES

_____

www.ingramcontent.com/pod-product-compliance
Lightning Source LLC
Chambersburg PA
CBHW041622120626
46551CB00003B/546

* 9 7 9 8 9 9 9 8 6 8 2 1 1 7 *